T0154689

Paul's Records

How a Refugee from the Vietnam War
Found Success Selling Vinyl
on the Streets of Hong Kong

text and photographs by
Andrew S. Guthrie

Paul's Records
ISBN 978-988-13764-3-5

© 2015 Andrew S. Guthrie
www.localidea.com

Published by Blacksmith Books
Room 26, 19/F, Block B,
Wah Lok Industrial Centre,
37-41 Shan Mei St., Fo Tan, Hong Kong
Tel: (+852) 2877 7899
www.blacksmithbooks.com

Contents

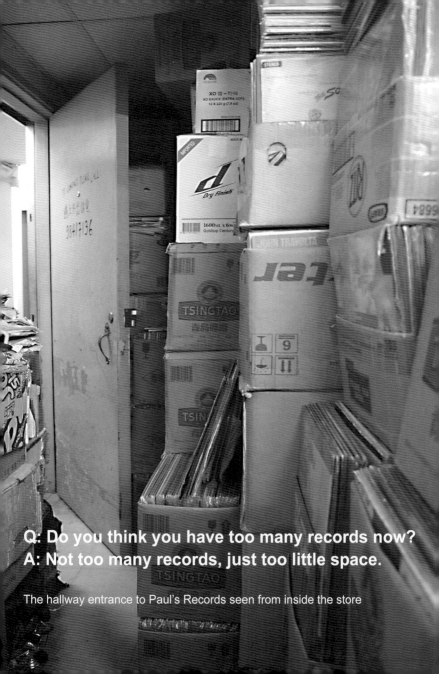

Q: Do you think you have too many records now?
A: Not too many records, just too little space.

The hallway entrance to Paul's Records seen from inside the store

How I Found A Record Store

When you travel a long way from home, especially when you know you will be gone for a long time (or never return) you might bring along a placeholder (an object that can be carried), a relic from that distant place; that place that will, forever after, always turn up in your dreams.

Shortly after I arrived in Hong Kong in 2005, I began to search for second-hand vinyl record stores. This is the way I began to familiarize myself in the unknown city. I was also holding onto the obsolete past – the analog recordings and attendant packaging that I had grown up with and that had been replaced by the binary code and its invisible form.

Nevertheless, a market for vinyl records still exists, a kind of antique market that can found somewhere, somehow, in most cities of the world (if not actually in abundance). I knew what these plastic recordings looked like and what I might discover when I sorted through them – a pile that might contain some pleasant and unexpected sound, or conversely, another familiar but welcomed addition to my catalog.

Even so, I was already traveling with my own stacks

– I had packed a collection of about 500 seven-inch singles. I reasoned that the 45rpms would be lighter than the leaden crates of LPs that I had left behind. Now, in the unfamiliar surroundings of Hong Kong, I looked for the smaller of the two disc sizes in order to hear the foreign city's sound while relying on the intuition and well-practiced routines that I had picked up from years of collecting.

One of my first stops was Collectables in Central, Hong Kong. I can no longer recall what led me to that location, where I picked up the directions, or what scent I was following. These are the talents of the collector (or "amateur enthusiast") that seem inexplicable to the outsider (to the casual rather than true fanatic). The uninitiated frequently asks: how did you find that? And how is it that you can rattle off all the band members' names (let alone where they ended up)?

Perhaps I had already been digging in the moldy confines of the Cat Street junk shops (in Sheung Wan). Here there were actual piles of stuff crammed into metal street market booths (common to Hong Kong), piles that would slowly spill into the street; lusciously decrepit avalanches that included everything from rusty Zippo lighters, to brittle Cantonese opera promotions, to cheap jewelry, to half-broken toys, to (finally) the occasional 45rpm.

When I first came upon Collectables, in its walk-up location (a building without elevators) it occupied two floors but was in the process of reducing its overhead. On the top floor (where stock was being deleted) there was also an impressive (and actual) pile, an accumulation that I probably could have crawled under (or been suffocated by). Here I could rummage at cut-rate prices, though I was expending labor by having to set aside the endless "hits", ubiquitous songs and singers that gave me an inkling of Hong Kong's long-gone musical interests. I began to understand why Nat King Cole holds a significant place in some of Wong Kar Wai's films.

As some of you may well know, in the over-arching pursuit of consumption, the savvy shopper can be as devious as the entrepreneur, so at first I would say nothing to KY Chan (who was then operating Collectables) about the possible value of singles that I found in that top-floor pile and was buying at cut rate. But eventually, this competitive relationship eased; I was seeking an informant; we were united by our common obsession.

It was the local market that I wanted to know more

9

about; not the international conglomerates that had dumped Engelbert Humperdinck, Cliff Richard and Tom Jones all over Hong Kong, but the local subsidiaries or home-grown labels that had produced their version of modernism in the form of rock and roll simulacra or in the standardized melding of "east meets west".

Eventually, KY Chan lent me seven LPs to display at an exhibition I organized at the store Kapok called "Pop I.D." I asked him to select and explain some "important" local releases. He came up with both an eclectic and obvious combination that included Sam Hui and Teddy Robin along with an obscure avant-garde rock band (蟬 or Cicada) and something representative of KY's preferred genre, "Folk-Rock".

"Pop I.D." was also a release party for my edition "Broken Records: 1960-1969". I had solicited music-related artwork to display at the release party through a classified ad in HK Magazine and William Fung wrote to ask if he could exhibit his Reggae records/CDs and memorabilia collection - an unusual approach, not only for the blending of consumer and/ or producer, but also because Reggae is a fairly unappreciated genre among Hong Kong people. It was

William who first took me to Paul's Records (among other places).

Now I realize I don't know Paul's last name (or in Chinese, his family name). When Paul was selling records on the street, he was also known as "The Bearded Guy"(鬚鬚仔). But if I don't know his family name, he is still easy to identify. He is what he does: Paul's Records.

Sadly, Mr. Chan (of Collectables) died from brain cancer in 2009. I am truly indebted to him, not only for what is cited above, but also for his highly receptive attitude towards my interests and ambitions, not to mention the generous discounts he gave me.

"Pop I.D." took place on April 6 – May 6, 2007, when Kapok was located near Tin Hau Temple Road in Tai Hang, Hong Kong. Special thanks to Arnault Castel, owner/operator

(from Wikipedia) Samuel Hui Koon-kit (born 1948), usually known as Sam Hui, is a Hong Kong Cantopop singer, lyricist and film actor. He is credited with popularizing Cantopop both with the infusion of Western-style music and using popular, street Cantonese jargon in his lyrics. Hui is considered by some to be the first major superstar of Cantopop.

(from Wikipedia) Kwan Wai-pang (born 1945) better known as Teddy Robin, is a Hong Kong pop singer-songwriter, actor, and director. He began his music career in the 1960s when Hong Kong English pop was at its peak in terms of popularity in Hong Kong. He led a band named Teddy Robin and the Playboys.

"Broken Records: 1960 – 1969" available from Printed Matter

HK Magazine is a free weekly English-language magazine published in Hong Kong

(Paul) Au Tak Shing, 歐德成

The cramped interior of Paul's Records, March, 2013

Sample Record #1. Poon Sow Keng （潘秀瓊）

Paul: This is a record from Hong Kong on the Five Continent label. Poon Sow Keng was born in Malaysia but moved to Singapore when she was young. She sings in the Shanghai style, kind of jazzy songs sung in Mandarin. I won't sell this one because the cover artwork is very rare, very unusual, and in good condition.

"Shanghai Style" is really not one type of music (though you know it when you hear it) but generally refers to the kind of music produced in Shanghai from the 1930s onward. The city at that time was an international hub with many dance and music nightclubs that resulted in a nascent recording industry.

Sample Record #2. Lui Hung (呂紅)

Paul: This is by the daughter of a very famous local Hong Kong composer and band leader from the 50s and 60s (Lui Man Sing). It's on the Diamond label, a major Hong Kong label in the 1960s. Her records are now very expensive, about HK$500. The music is very Chinese, "Temple Street style", like in the cabarets in Yau Ma Tei (Kowloon).

"Temple Street Style" indicates traditional Chinese Folk melodies in which the lyrics were changed to reflect the lifestyle and conditions of the average Cantonese person in Hong Kong in the 1960s and 1970s. Originally, musicians would set up outdoors in the square in front of the temple in Yau Ma Tei (off of Temple Street). They were eventually forced from that location into nearby clubs, which still exist to this day.

The hallway and door of Paul's Records

Entrepreneurial Strategies

1.

Paul's Records is located in Sham Shui Po, a section of the Kowloon peninsula generally cited as one of the poorest neighborhoods in Hong Kong. Regardless of the income disparity being experienced by the average resident of Sham Shui Po, the area is attractive, vibrant and well worth visiting, being home to (among other things) many wholesale and retail clothing and fabric markets.

Sham Shui Po came into its own after the British colonial government, upon winning Hong Kong Island in 1842 as a result of the first opium war, began pushing their acquisitions further north. Originally, the Qing Dynasty had only ceded Hong Kong Island but eventually the British acquired all of the territory in Kowloon, even beyond Lion Rock mountain, an area that eventually ended at the Chinese border at Lo Wu. This part of the British colony has ever since been designated as "The New Territories".

Sham Shui Po sits southwest of Lion Rock, and was part of one of the first British demands for a larger buffer zone between Hong Kong Island and China

("The Mainland") for reasons of "security". In fact (as is per usual in these cases) part of the impetus for the colonial government's "security concerns" were the economic competition generated by businesses in the non-British territories that were siphoning off customers from Hong Kong Island. Some of these businesses even provided ferry services from Hong Kong for those who wanted to patronize Kowloon's bars, opium dens, and stores that were selling the cheaper goods that had been smuggled in from China.

All of Hong Kong and Kowloon was eventually handed back (the "hand-over") to China in 1997, as originally stipulated in the 1898 ninety-nine year British/Chinese lease. By that time, Sham Shui Po had well established its contemporary feel and purpose - a gritty, densely populated area that saw the kind of entrepreneurial innovation generated by a less affluent demographic. This economic mode can perhaps be best exemplified by the famous Apliu Street market, one of the few remaining areas of Hong Kong that still widely maintains its once ubiquitous "street stalls", green metal booths of about fifty square feet that sit right off of the sidewalk's curb.

The street stalls of Apliu Street are jam-packed with a variety of goods, everything from computer accessories, to clocks, to colorful electric lighting, to toys and knick-knacks and on to clothing and household goods. The market has a historical reputation as a "thieves market", a condition that is perhaps slightly over-blown by today's standards. Nevertheless, on one visit a few years ago, I was able to buy a "brand new" French-made DVD/VCD player chosen from a hastily built stack of boxes for one hundred Hong Kong dollars (about ten Euros or twelve US dollars).

Piles of used tools for sale on Apliu Street

Another aspect of the area that coincides with the eccentric collecting and organizing methods of Paul's Records (which I will get to in a moment) is its significant secondary or used-goods market, an anomaly in Hong Kong as economic status is stereotypically measured by way of the consumption of the newest of the new, while the slightly old is quickly discarded. There are many street stalls on Apliu Street that overflow with banged and battered

Typical street stall on Apliu Street

kitchen appliances, antique electronics, used DVDs and even the occasional box of LPs. This contrary sensibility and homage to the down and out, and otherwise discarded, is provided a proper celebratory

Looking down Apliu Street, Sham Shui Po

Apliu Street, Sham Shui Po

Apliu Street, Sham Shui Po

Sham Shui Po

Stone phallic charm
9cm / HK$60

Chinese coin
3cm / HK$10

Scratching ceramic monkey
5cm / HK$25

Bead figure
9cm / HK$40

Faux sushi pork floss bun
9cm / HK$7.5

Objects purchased in Sham Shui Po - 2014

Sham Shui Po

festival once a year when, during the first days of the Lunar New Year, everyone and anyone is allowed to pull whatever it is into the street in an attempt to turn their lead into gold.

2.

Paul began his full-fledged career as a seller of used records on these very same streets. Though currently and occasionally harshly discouraged by a governmental regulatory force, the entrepreneurial legacy of Hong Kong that allows someone to simply set up shop in whatever space is open and free is still easy to deduce. One can still find back alley open-air barbershops or a D.I.Y. shoe repair stand sandwiched between two "legitimate" storefronts.

This part of Paul's career is explained in his own words in another section of this book, so perhaps it would be best to explain here why, with all the other used record stores in Hong Kong (and there are a few, if in fact many), I would be drawn to document Paul's.

Paul is legendary among Hong Kong (and indeed, international) aficionados who seek out this product from the past that refuses to go away, including those

陳寶珠唱

興發影業公司出品　電影插曲原聲帶

Sample Record #3:
Connie Chan Po Chu（陳寶珠）

Connie Chan Po Chu is one of the most legendary Hong Kong actresses and singers of the 1960s. She is known for playing roles that Hong Kong's "factory girls" could identify with, that is, the working class women of that era who were employed by Hong Kong's booming manufacturing industries.

Her background in entertainment began at a young age which saw her steeped in both Cantonese and Peking Opera. She first appeared professionally on the stage at the age of nine. This background eventually led to her extensive film career, which at first saw her in roles that referred to or were directly inspired by traditional operas or by Chinese historical legends.

But she was savvy enough to shift with the times and adapt her style into the contemporary milieu, which, while still evoking a hardcore Cantonese sensibility, saw her crossover into the youth or "A-Go-Go" market. These movies also had, as would be expected, a romantic element that repeatedly paired her with the male lead, Lui Kei. In addition, she was cast in a few "female James Bond" movies, which allowed the local market to cash in on this international trend. The 45rpm pictured here is from one such movie, entitled "Lady Bond (aka Ladies in Distress)" contemporaries (and most especially the homemade and professional DJs) who have come to be known as "crate diggers". This reputation rests largely on word-of-mouth as Paul, while making some recent concessions, continues to remain, for the most part, "pre-digital". He has no email address, no website, no Ebay or Alibaba (the Chinese equivalent of Ebay) and his Facebook page was started and is administered by another like-minded fan.

Paul steps across stacks of records to get around his shop

You can roll up to the door of Paul's shop (which is also his residence) and give his doorbell a ring, but it is a good idea to give him a phone call before you arrive.

This is not to say that there aren't any references to Paul on the web, as countless individuals have blogged about their visits and purchases, visitors from both inside and outside of Hong Kong. But it is Paul's particular story (which again, I will mostly leave to his own words), along with his welcoming personality, his fluent tri-lingualism in English, Cantonese, and Putonghua/Mandarin, and his unique organizing strategies that provoke the documentary impulse.

Paul demonstrating his unique record cleaning method which is done as the record spins, playing out its pops or skips. Spraying a 50/50 mixture of alcohol and water (or straight water) onto the record, he then runs his finger along the surface or lets the turntable's needle run through the mixture. Paul refers to this as "removing fossils". He also says, "It's like a railroad track that is rusty and then it rains and the train runs over the wet track and squeezes out the rust and residue".

As can be noted in the photographs here, Paul is a hoarder, always willing to accept or purchase more and more records; to stack box upon box into a seemingly unfathomable mass. His total collection (which not only includes his store in Sham Shui Po, but a storage space in Tuen Mun) supposedly exceeds 50,000 records, in addition to countless music-related books, memorabilia, and electronic playback equipment. Unlike most record stores, in which the product would be neatly sectioned off into respective genres, to find the desired item the customer must ask Paul, "Where is the...?" or, "Do you have any...?" Amazingly, Paul can usually locate something along the requested lines, if not today, then sometime soon.

These conditions, which mean that the actual space that the customer can stand within is minimal, also lead to unplanned for, yet significant side effects. In the first place, if there are other customers there that block your already limited movement, you, the customer, are left to investigate whatever is immediately before you, and while some boxes have some kind of organizing method, you might come across something quite unexpected and personally valuable in a box supposedly dedicated to something you would otherwise have nothing to do with.

I am the adventurous shopper, who no longer or rarely asks Paul for something specific. At Paul's Records,

I know what I am looking for when it finds me. In this way, I fall back on my own thoughts about recorded music. I am inside my head (though I share the knowledge of what I've found with anyone who will listen). But given the limitations of personal space at Paul's, I also interact with my fellow customer, that is, whoever is there in that small space at any given moment. I ask them where they are from, what they are looking for, how they found out about Paul's Records.

If you ask, Paul will play any record you are considering buying. This is the other seemingly unintended side effect of the architecture of Paul's Records. One listens to, talks about, or keeps quiet about, your fellow customers' requests. Both of you, or two or three, stand in front of Paul who cues the room's central turntable (sound system). You are in an apartment building in Sham Shui Po; in a fifth-floor, two-bedroom flat crammed with flat, circular, black vinyl records. There is about ten square feet of standing space between you and the piles of records.

This is the way you (the way we used to) listen to vinyl records – it's a bit like sitting around a campfire while someone tells a story. But there should be no mistaking that while we are consuming music in a way that can be differentiated from digital media (where frequently the listener is solitarily absorbed in his or her headphones) we are still involved with a kind of robot (the record and the record player), but in the case of Paul's Records, all the variables involved in this particular pursuit – the neighborhood, the venue, the jumble of boxes, the confined space and of course, Paul – combine to create an experience worth documenting.

In spite of the clutter within Paul's Records, he has divided the space between "Chinese records" on the right-hand side and "Western records" on the left. This photograph is of the corner containing "Chinese records".

Paul: They called him "The Oriental Elvis" not so much be cause of the music style, but because he was singing tradi tional melodies with contemporary lyrics. He tried to look handsome. He was tall and thin. Maybe he wasn't a sex sym bol like Elvis Presley but he was always singing flirty songs. Cheng Kwun Min was in the top rank of Hong Kong entertain ers in the 1960s. They would do things like use the melody o "Three Coins in the Fountain" and then add Cantonese lyrics At that time it was very easy to make money this way. Let me show you something funny. (shows record cover) The Orien tal Elvis. (record cover copies style and layout of Elvis gold album). This came out around '64. At that time they had a lot of movies with these songs in them, black and white mov es, low-budget productions. In the 1960s in Hong Kong there were lot of guys dressing like Elvis, flirting with girls. These guys were not educated, could not speak English, so they made the local Hong Kong version of that attitude, they made songs with Chinese lyrics that gave that attitude. They also would make a kind of modern Cantonese Opera. They would use the traditional melodies but put funny words about the contemporary lifestyle. They would arrange the music so it could be played on saxophone, drums, electric guitar. So the people who sing in those productions wouldn't dress in the traditional Cantonese Opera outfits; men would dress in mod ern suits or the ladies in mini-dresses. Cheng Kwun Min was singing a lot of this kind of stuff. He had one very funny song about flirting with a Chinese bar girl in Wan Chai called "Suzie Wong"; he pretends to be an American G.I. who is on leave in Wan Chai. "Suzie Wong" is one of the girls sitting outside the bar in Wan Chai. Back then (in the Wan Chai bars) they were all Chinese, local Chinese girls. The style of the song is "East Meets West", traditional melody with contemporary lyrics. In the song Cheng Kwun Min occasionally uses English phrases like "What's your name?" He died in the 1990s completely broke but he had earned a lot of money before that and was very famous. The Chinese in Singapore and Thailand would know him by the name "The Oriental Elvis" but he was really famous in Hong Kong. Even so, he died penniless.

It is said that the Chinese have five bad habits (counting on fingers): Prostitution, Gambling, Drinking (wine), Loafing (lazy), Smoking (opium). In the '60s they had many funny songs about these habits to educate the people. But it was more fun to listen to them than to be educated by them. People listen to these songs a lot but they never change. So, Cheng Kwun Min gambled a lot and lost a lot of money. And he always had a lot of women and they would always be asking him for money. So he died broke. Someone told me that he saw him when he was really old pushing a trolley in Mong Kok picking up cardboard and cans (for recycling).

Paul

You ask me how I started and why I was interested in this kind of business, why I was so hooked and passionate about records. I tell interviewers that I'm still living in the seventies . . . I have not had enough fun yet, because in the seventies I was riding Chopper bicycles, listening to Deep Purple, Led Zeppelin, going to a lot of parties, street fighting, drinking beer . . . we were wearing bell-bottoms, high-heeled sneakers in the street, riding the bicycles . . . that was in Vietnam, '73/'74 . . . in '73 I was 16 years old. I was born in '57.

Paul (on left) with his younger brothers, Saigon, 1969

. . . in the early seventies the Vietnam War was still going on and I had a lot of friends who were in bands, in rock and roll bands, garage bands, stuff like that and we would share information, and at that time, because of the Vietnam War, some of the US charity organizations brought in a lot of used clothing from the States, and those were "hippie" clothing, like Levis jeans, like the clothing CCR (Creedence Clearwater Revival) was wearing . . . so my friends told me "Hey, they are selling the new fashions on the streets", the styles of the early seventies were being sold on the streets, they had stolen them from these charities, so my friends and I were like "Wow!", because they were not selling these kind of fashions in Vietnam, as the originals were actually very expensive. Sometimes we would have our own versions hand-tailored, but now we could get these used clothes and sometimes they were in quite good condition . . . things like shirts with flared sleeves. Suddenly, a lot of people were selling this kind of clothing and my friends and I went there and bought a lot of them for very cheap.

In '72 I was 15 but I had some neighbors who were a few years older and they were always hiding in their homes because at that time there was a (military) draft for whomever was 18 or older . . . so these neighbors were hiding all the time in their houses. They would not go out into the streets. But the Vietnam government knew about that (draft dodgers), so sometimes in the middle of the night there would be a search. They would surround the houses and one by one search these houses, trying to catch them.

At first they would put them in a Boot Camp for a few

months and then into the battlefield and of course a lot of them died. I can still remember that I would be talking to my elder neighbors, joking with them, and then they would be taken off and then I would hear they had been killed. So, it wasn't going to be long before I was going to be drafted (in '75), so my parents began to worry.

At that time they wanted me to learn Vietnamese . . . if you wanted to avoid the draft it would be because your eyesight was bad, or you had a profession like professor, or you could take an examination that showed that you were part of the elite. But this examination was in Vietnamese and I could hardly speak Vietnamese because I had grown up in China-town (in Saigon at that time). I had been speaking only Chinese since the time I was born . . . Cantonese, the Hong Kong style, because my parents were from Southern China. They called this the examination for the elites, for those people with higher education, so, because this examination was in Vietnamese and I hardly knew Vietnamese, when I was 15 my parents started having me instructed in Vietnamese, but that was too late and I wasn't able to learn on a high level, so, a lot of my older neighbors were being smuggled out of Vietnam and sent to Hong Kong. My mother began to arrange this for me.

Perhaps you could bribe someone to get a false ID that falsified your age, making you appear younger than 18. If you were naughty and got into trouble in the streets and the police looked at those fake documents and did not believe them, then they would say, "Oh, you're 18, come with me . . .", and then take you to a boot camp, but then they might also say, "We can make a deal. I like your Rolex watch . . . etc", and then they would let you go.

Paul (on left) with his youngest brother, Saigon, 1971

The Chinatown in Saigon was huge, like three or four districts in Hong Kong (from Tsim Sha Tsui to Mei Foo). We had never left Chinatown since the day I was born.

When I was living in Saigon, from '72 to '75, I was listening to this (western pop) music on AFVN (American Forces Vietnam Network) just like they did in the movie, Good Morning Vietnam. It was on FM radio, but FM radio was banned (for Vietnamese citizens). FM radios were only available in the PX (Post Exchange), the store that was only open to the American GIs. So FM radios were illegal, but they were smuggled out and were available on the streets. FM radios were illegal because the VC (Viet Cong) could listen to them and maybe get information about what the Americans were doing. But my friends had one (an FM radio) and I spent a lot of time with them listening to The Beach Boys, Sonny and Cher, The Ventures, and Motown, Country and Western . . .

I couldn't quite understand the English but we had some lyrics books, and sometimes on the records they had the lyrics. We liked the music, but we didn't understand the words, so we always had a dictionary. That's how we learned English. And also there was the AFVN television channel and we watched that every night.

It was all right for Vietnamese to watch the AFVN TV. It was for the American soldiers, but if the Vietnamese citizens had a TV it was OK to watch everyday. So every Monday we had Combat, on Tuesday Rawhide, on Wednesday and Thursday Batman, Friday Gunsmoke. They wanted to make the American GIs feel at home, so we watched the same things you were watching in the States, not long after they had aired the same episodes. But it was all in black and white.

When I was in secondary school my classmates had a friend who was a Vietnamese hippie. He played drums in a band. He was about four or five years older than I was. His band played Iron Butterfly songs and Grand Funk Railroad songs. He had a lot of American records that had been smuggled out of the Post Exchange (the store only for American GIs). It was illegal because these records were stolen goods, but they were being sold in the street.

So I was used to American music, because at that time it was like living in a kind of small America as the U.S. had been in Vietnam for so long. We were brought up watching the U.S. television and we were surrounded by American culture. In Saigon there were a lot of bars that were frequented by American GIs. A lot of them were like hippie-types, even though their hair had been cut. During the late '60s a lot of the stores on the street level were turned into bars for American GIs. The MPs (military police) were always patrolling them as a lot of times there would be fights between black and white GIs. A lot of big hotels

Sample Record #5:
Lee Yin Ping (李燕萍)

Paul: Lee Yin Ping started her own record company and lost a lot of money. She was very strict and wanted the records and the cover art to be very good, the printing to be very good. And so she did not have money left to invest in property and when she died she was very broke. She came to me because she wanted me to buy some of her leftover records. She sold them to me even if she lost money, she sold me the new records at a very cheap price. I have respect for her. These are still popular among the old Chinese, those who are 70 or 80 years old now. These records originally came out in the early '70s. (Sing along with the records) This song is for the New Year – the lyrics are about **riches, nobility, and honor.**

She was also in some movies and starred in some local TV series in the mid-70s. I like her because we were the same kind of people, devoted to music, perhaps too devoted to music. We would rather spend our money on music, not to exploit music for the money.

She was famous for one song. The song was a traditional Cantonese melody and they created new lyrics for it. She was the first one to make that song popular The song was about handsome boys, or something like that. First she addresses the boy, calling him pretty boy ("leng" in Cantonese), then she sings, "You attract me and I am always thinking about you". It's like a flirting song.

She lived in Yau Ma Tei, around Temple Street for a very long time. Everyone around there knows her. She was very famous in Temple Street, a Cantonese Opera star. Maybe not the biggest, maybe a second line-star in Cantonese Opera. She invited me for tea at her flat in Yau Ma Tei once. It was a walk-up (no elevator), a very old building, and she was renting her flat. She had boxes of her records in the kitchen and it was very wet in there and they were also getting destroyed by termites. She said to me, "Hey, you are selling records maybe you can try to sell some of these. Maybe you can buy some of these from me." She said, "Look, Paul, I am living in this crappy apartment, paying high rent, because I was so strict (had high standards) for my record company." She hired local Chinese musicians who charged by the hour and she also rented the studio. There was no multi-tracks then so everything had to be done in many takes. I respected her so I bought a lot of her records. There are hundreds of them in my storage space. They are brand new, unopened albums and I sell them for about HK$60 each.

were completely booked by GIs as well and these became targets for Viet Cong bombings, they just would throw some bombs or run a truck load of dynamite in there.

I liked western music, including the stuff coming from Britain because I was more used to it. My neighbors listened to a lot of local Vietnamese pop music and I got used to that style as well, whether I really liked it or not, it became part of my memories. The Chinese in Saigon were listening to a lot of records from Hong Kong and Taiwan. They were getting records from Hong Kong as soon as they came out. A lot of entertainers from Hong Kong and Taiwan came to perform in Saigon. But my preference was always for Western music.

It was not very common for us boys to be interested in American rock music, because most of the Chinese in Chinatown could hardly speak English. But in fact some of the schools for Chinese were English-language schools. This made them slightly more expensive, and we would sometimes have Western teachers. Sometimes even GIs would come and teach us English. They would come in their uniforms and put their M16 rifles in the corner while they were teaching.

The big record companies may have thought there was no market in Saigon, but in fact we were buying Taiwanese bootlegs of all those hit albums. There was also no major label distribution in Taiwan, so they set up different bootleg labels. They would just copy the whole thing, the record and the jacket. At that time there were also a lot of local bands that played in the bars in Saigon. They were all probably on drugs. They were covering CCR, Santana, The Carpenters, all the American Top 40 songs.

Besides that, we were also reading American magazines like Playboy and Penthouse. Those magazines were sold only to American GIs but we would find them around, sometimes in the flea markets. So all those American things, including the Choppers, the motorcycles and the fashions - that is what I started picking up on and being influenced by around 1972 or so. My parents hated that stuff. They were always telling me that it was junk, that "those people had long hair and were on drugs . . . we should not listen to them."

My father was born in 1913 and when he was a small boy, around ten years old, my grandfather brought him and his brothers from Guangdong, Sihui, China（廣東四會）to Saigon, Vietnam. My grandfather was very rich at that time. Airplanes were not common then, so they came to Vietnam by sea route. And my mother, because of the Communist take-over of China, came first to Macau and later in the early 1950s, she came to Vietnam. My grandfather on my mother's side had some connections with the big bosses

of gambling in Macau. They wanted to set up similar businesses in Vietnam, so my mother's father came to Saigon. But my grandfather could not make the right connections in Vietnam, so that business My father was an accountant in the late sixties, but later he became a receptionist in a hotel, which was very near our home. At one point, very suddenly, the whole hotel was booked by American GIs. Then my

A typical "bootleg" 10" 33 1/3 rpm record made in Hong Kong in the late 1960s containing unlicensed American and British pop hits, with its generic and seemingly incongruous jacket (opposite page), probably (again) a bootlegged calendar picture of Singapore. There is a handwritten number written in the top right of the jacket (above the "label") that would correspond to a list of songs that would be available in the store. Many different "playlists" would be packaged in the same generic jacket.

father was promoted to manager of the Chinese restaurant in that hotel. It was a very big hotel and the owner was a very famous man in Chinatown.

There was only warfare directly in Saigon during the Chinese New Year in 1968 (the Tet Offensive). In '68 I was only 11 years old. The Viet Cong started to smuggle guns into the city starting in '67 and then on the days of the Chinese New Year they used the sound from firecrackers going off to cover the sound of gunfire. On the morning of the second day of the New Year suddenly there was a curfew and the news spread that the Viet Cong were in Saigon and for weeks there was war going on inside the city. In the nighttime I could see jets firing tracer bullets that looked like red dots, and I could see lots of bombing and burning going on across the river. The adults were very worried but we kids thought it was funny, like, "Oh good, curfew, now we don't have to go to school . . ."

I have a half brother, maybe 11 or 12 years older than I was, and I have three younger brothers, but in 1975 I would turn 18 so I would be the first one to go. But in '73/'74 I was already drafted into the neighborhood vigilante force, which was like a neighborhood watch. That happened before you were18, not old enough for the army, when you were about

<u>WINTER WORLD OF LOVE</u> - by Engelbert Humperdinck

My love, the days are colder, so let me take your hand
and lead you through a snow-white land Oh, oh, oh, oh
my love the year is older - So let me hold you tight and
while away this winter night oh, oh. I see the fire-
light in your eyes - Come kiss me now before it dies.
We'll find a winter world of love - 'Cause love is warmer
in December, My darling stay here in my arms 'till summer
comes along. And in our winter world of love you'll see
we always will remember that as the snow lay on the ground
we found our winter world of love. Because the nights
are longer, We'll have the time to say such tender things
before each day Oh, oh, oh, oh and then when love is
stronger - Perhaps you'll give your heart and promise me
we'll never part oh, no. And at the end of every year -
I'll be so glad to have you near. We'll find a winter
world of love 'Cause love is warmer in December, My darling
stay here in my arms 'till summer comes along. And in our
winter of love you'll see we always will remember that as
the snow lay on the ground we found our winter world of
love . . . .

Occasionally, wedged into the sleeves of 1960s and 1970s 45 rpms found in Hong Kong, one comes across meticulous hand-made lyric sheets (such as the above). One day, when Paul and I were chatting about these curious artifacts it occurred to both of us that these were propbably auto-didactic English language learning materials. This one has even been signed by the original owner, probably using his "English name", a name that was usually assigned to a pupil by a school's English teacher. Such is also the case with Paul's "name".

Sample Record #6:
"Car Owner" (soundtrack from 1966 movie)

Paul: A flexi-disc EP soundtrack of a comedy aimed at car-owning snobs in 1960s Hong Kong. One track uses the melody of "Love Potion Number 9" with three people singing lyrics that say things like, "I work as a clerk in a bad company with a no-good accountant who didn't give me my $1000 commission. If I am angry with him, he will delay further . . . I'm worried about paying the installments on the car . . ."

Hong Kong 's version of middle class ambition circa mid-1960s, under the specifics of Hong Kong's overworked, underpaid staff employees starring the veteran Hong Kong actors (from top to bottom) Cheung Ying-Tsoi (張英才) , Teresa Ha Ping (夏萍) , and Leung Sing-Bo (梁醒波)

15 or 16. They gave you a black uniform and an old carbine (rifle), not an M16 or a tommy gun like the GIs had.

I can still remember one evening when hundreds of us (in the vigilante force) were in the school yard and an instructor was carrying around a carbine, telling us how to operate and clean the gun and I hardly understood him because he was speaking Viet-namese. So in fact, it was dan-gerous as most of us really didn't understand how to handle the ri-fle.

From Paul's personal collection - a 7" EP of "Khong" by Khanhly

They had a sched-ule and if it was your turn you would have to spend the night on watch, it was like a neighborhood watch, at a post that was like a small police station or a community hall. I would have to do it about every two weeks. The carbine guns would be there, guns that were from the 1940s or 1950s, maybe American guns from WWII. They gave you the black uniform and a gun and you would spend the night on watch. Most of the boys in the vigilante force were quite young, about 15 or 16 years old.

But what happened was that the boys (in the vigilante forces) would engage in trouble, not battle! These teenage boys would carry the guns and sometimes shoot them at someone they were having trouble with in the neighborhood. When it was my turn, I would have to spend the whole night there, but we would be eating, talking, hanging out.

We were all living in this Chinatown, and a lot of the Chinese boys were like me. Most of us

One of the most popular Vietnamese hits of the early 70s, covered by Taiwanese, Singaporean and Hong Kong artists.

could hardly speak Vietnamese, but some of us could. There were about four schools in Vietnam that were for Chinese. The Vietnamese would not go to these schools, because if you would go to this school everyone would be speaking Cantonese. Also, if a Vietnamese would go there, they would be discriminated against by the Chinese boys, not beaten up, but it was kind of a racialized environment. In fact this school is just like a "China inside of Vietnam." Of course the Vietnamese didn't like that. I can remember once there was an Indian girl, this small teenage Indian girl who came to our school and she was really discriminated against; she would get bullied and teased and whatever.

Since '72, after Nixon visited China, the Americans had started to withdraw their forces. I can remember in '73 the AFVN TV channel closed. In '75, in late April, Saigon fell, but I had left before that. I got to Hong Kong in February of '75.

I was smuggled out of Vietnam a few months after my 17th birthday. I was getting very close to the draft age. The next year I would reach the draft age. My mother arranged everything for me to be smuggled out of Vietnam. Until this day I don't know exactly how she arranged all that. We had a relative on my father's side living in a rural area outside of Saigon and that is where we went before we got on the ship. I went with a cousin of mine. He spoke Vietnamese because he lived in a Vietnamese district, but his Chinese was very poor. It was arranged that we would be smuggled out together.

A little while after Christmas 1974 we were told to go to this rural area to wait for a week or two until the smugglers had arranged everything. My cousin and I took a taxi out of Saigon, but after about ten minutes or so, we were stopped by a policeman because at that time a lot of police and soldiers would line the side of the road looking for boys around our age. If they saw someone around the draft age they would blow the whistle and tell them to stop and ask for their IDs. If you tried to run away they would shoot in the air to alert the other soldiers. So this policeman asked for our IDs, looked at them very carefully and I could see that he was very disappointed that we were just a little younger than the draft age. I could see that in his face. If we had been the right age and had no other papers saying that we shouldn't be drafted, then they would take you right then. They would send you right to the boot camp.

So we continued on our way and got to a farmhouse. I was living there for a few weeks and I was very lonely, very impatient, and I was very naughty chasing the farm animals around. My relatives really hated that I was doing that. Occasionally my fathers and my brothers would come to visit me. After a couple of weeks my relatives took my cousin and myself to another area nearer Saigon and told us to wait for a van that would be driven by a lady. We were supposed to get in the van and she would take us to the next stage of the trip. A lady wearing sunglasses drove by and signaled to us,and I don't know why, but we didn't get in the van. We mistook her for someone else. So then we had to wait another week.

Finally we were taken to an area called Vung Tau, a beach area near Saigon. My family used to go there to go swimming; it's about one or two hours' drive from Saigon. We were taken to another farmhouse near there and had to wait another two weeks. There were many other people waiting to be smuggled out who were staying in different houses in this village. This was a village of about ten houses that were owned by Vietnamese peasants and each house was holding 20 or 30 people who were waiting to be smuggled out. When we finally boarded this cargo ship, a Taiwanese cargo ship, I saw there were about 200 people total, and it wasn't just boys like me, but also women of different ages, probably from rich families.

Four days before the Chinese New Year in 1974, early 1975 in the Western calendar, we were suddenly told that we were leaving, so we walked down a path between the fields in complete darkness until we got to the seaside where we split up into groups of ten that boarded different sampans. These sampans took us to a fishing junk further out in the sea. These fishing boats went very fast, the sea was rough and they had hidden us in the engine room where there were all these fumes, so we were all throwing up. Finally we arrived at the cargo ship and I saw many other fishing junks arriving, waiting to load all the people. I had nothing with me, just a small bag with some clothes in it. As soon as we got on deck they sent us down to a hold where there were bags of rice all stacked up. This where we stayed and slept during the trip.

Paul's South Vietnam ID card

The next day we went up on the deck and walked around and I saw we were already under way, sailing on the South China Sea, going north towards Hong Kong. Some people had better places to sleep because they had gotten on board first, especially some of the women, some had cabins. I don't know if they paid more, but my family had paid about five taels of gold, or about HK$100,000 in today's money. The conditions on the ship weren't terrible, just very crowded with all the smuggled passengers plus the crew. We boys spent a lot of time walking around the deck, singing songs to amuse ourselves. It was wintertime

Sample Record #7: Midnight Jazz

This is the kind of record (at Paul's Records) that seems to find you, but it is also emblematic of what's available, specific and unique to the store. Jazz is not a genre very widely distributed at Paul's, in fact, among all the other boxes, there is only one dedicated to that genre (though, often enough, customers do ask for it). Paul has explained the availability of used jazz records in terms of class and the neighborhood's listening habits. Jazz will generally be more available in Central Hong Kong, where the more affluent collectors live (along with many western-ers) But if there is something special in the jazz mode in Sham Shui Po, Paul will proudly display it on top of the stacks of boxes.

But there is also (as we have already seen) a certain layer of "cheese" to Paul's collection, a charming brand of culturally specific presentation and packaging epitomized by the knock-off or bootleg, or in this case, a re-packaging of pre-existing American music for an Asian audience. When I first saw this paradoxi-cally garish yet attractive cover I was sure that it contained horrific bar/lounge instrumental versions of either movie soundtracks or pop tunes, but no, it con-

ミッドナイト・ジャス第2集

グリスビーのブルース
映画「現金に手を出すな」より
夜は千の眼を持つ
思い出の星影
酒とバラの日々
ポインシアナ

ブルース・マーチ
愚かなり我が心
素敵なあなた
私の心はパパのもの
オール・ナイト・ロング

バド・ジョンソン
ソニー・スティット
ラムゼイ・ルイス
アーマッド・ジャマル
ジーン・ショー
アート・ファーマー
ヘニー・コルソン
ケニー・バレル

tains reputable jazz musicians such as Sonny Stitt, Art Farmer and Benny Golson playing melodies that lean towards what the image on the record jacket implies – "Midnight Jazz" – mellow tunes for those uninitiated in the more avant-garde or progressive aspects of "African-American Classical Music". To put it another way (in the American idiom) the record contains "make-out music".

This is a Japanese produced compilation and, as Paul puts it, is the kind of product made especially for the stressed-out over-worked Japanese office worker, something "to take the edge off" (as it were, abetted with "Japanese Scotch"); a typical Japanese cultural appropriation, complete with the "right" female type under a Renoir print, signalling sleaze and sophistication. As further regards the semiotics of Japanese culture, it can also be noted that it is usually a good bet, that no matter how old the record (or the relative effects of acidic paper on the cover illustration), that if it was previously owned by a Japanese collector, the record itself will be exceptionally well taken care of.

and it was cold on the ship, but there was no bath because they had to conserve water. Some people could talk to the Taiwanese crew in Mandarin. They were smuggling for money but sympathetic that we Chinese would not want to fight and die for South Vietnam.

This cargo ship took four days to get to Hong Kong. On January 30th we arrived in international waters outside of Hong Kong, but because it was Chinese New Year, none of the Hong Kong fishermen wanted to come pick us up. We had to wait four more days, going around in circles. One of the Taiwanese crew became upset and pointed at the ship's smokestack and said that going round and round in circles was just like burning money.

All of us were getting bored and impatient, but finally on

Paul (front, June 2013)

the fourth day, around four or five o'clock, the Hong Kong junks arrived and started to pick us up. They were the Tanka fisher people of Hong Kong who spent their whole life on the ocean, and they spoke a different Chinese dialect from us. Once again, they hid us in the engine room. After an hour or so, just as the sky was getting dark, we got to the coastline of Hong Kong at Shek O. We actually had to jump from the junk into the water and wade up to the beach.

Paul (back, June 2013)

Once we got to the road we saw that there were many mini-buses waiting. Groups of 14 people would fill each mini-bus and go. When they got to us, there were no more mini-buses, so five of us got into a taxi. All those people, the mini-bus and taxi drivers were connected to the smuggling network.

The taxi took us to Wan Chai where I saw all these advertisements for products that I had never seen in Vietnam, things like ads for color TV, western products and all that. The taxi dropped us at an apartment building where we met this woman working for the smugglers who was about 40 years old. She took us up to a flat and told us to call our relatives. Those smugglers wouldn't do business with you unless they knew you had a relative in Hong Kong. They wanted to collect some more money from our relatives.

I took out the number of my uncle, my mother's brother, and called him. When he answered and I told him who I was he got very angry. Even though my mother must have told him we were coming, he was very upset that we were there. He was only living in one room of a flat in Wan Chai and he told me it was too late at night for him to pick me up, that his wife was at a mah jong game and that he was taking care of the children. He told me I would have to wait until tomorrow and he hung up the phone. The next day I talked to my aunt, who told the smuggler to bring my cousin and myself over to my uncle's place. The smuggler was very careful, and even though we weren't going far, she wouldn't let us walk on the street, so we took a taxi. When we got up to my uncle's house, my aunt paid the smugger HK$400 for both of us. At that time HK$400 was equal to about HK$10,000 now. It was noon on Sunday, and my uncle was working for a famous tailor in the Mandarin Hotel in Central, but he came back to the house to see us. He was very discouraging, telling us it was a very bad economic time in Hong Kong and wondering why we came to Hong Kong when the stock market was so bad. He said my mother was crazy for sending me there, that he was only living in this small room. My aunt was much nicer and told my uncle to take us to dim sum since it was Sunday.

At that time I did not have any money but I had these relatives in Hong Kong. My parents would send some money to me through them. All that was in 1975, 37 years ago. I'm still living in the '70s. 1975 was just like yesterday. At that time (1975) the law in Hong Kong was like this: you didn't have to carry your ID around. The cops would not track your ID on the street. They would ask you for your ID but if you said you had forgotten it, or whatever, they would let you go. It was illegal to hire people without papers but no one really checked. So, I had no papers or anything else, but I worked in a hotel that was owned by this Vietnamese-Chinese rich man. He was one of my classmate's uncles. I had happened to run into this classmate in Hong Kong and he made an introduction for me. I worked there for a year.

About ten weeks after we had arrived in Hong Kong, Saigon fell. After that, in August we reported ourselves to the police. But before Saigon fell, if they would catch you, they might send you back to Saigon.

After the fall of Saigon the rest of my family tried to escape. A lot of people were trying to escape. My parents and brothers went to the American Embassy because we had a cousin who worked for the Americans, they tried to use that connection, but a lot of people were crowding in there. You've seen the news photos. But they were not lucky enough to escape, so they stayed there. And that worried the hell out of me. They waited seven years and then in '83 they were able to go to Canada. We had an uncle in Canada who helped them apply for refugee status there. They took a flight first to Hong Kong, and then were transferred to a flight to Canada, so I didn't see them at that time.

I worked in the hotel in Hong Kong for a year and then I started working in a supermarket owned by another rich Viet-

Paul selling records on the streets of Sham Shui Po (from article in Hong Kong Daily News,1985)

namese/Chinese. At that time I was very naughty, and people always complained about me. I was playing more than working, chasing cats, fooling around. So they fired me after a year. It was '77 and I was 20. So then I started working in a jeans shop, a place that was selling bell-bottom jeans; the fashions of the time. In '78 people were dressing like John Travolta. I dressed like that because I loved the lifestyle, the rock culture, you know, the fashions, the movies, the records. I worked at the jeans shop for one year and then I quit again and started working in a shop that sold musical instruments in Central.

None of my jobs lasted long. Either I would quit or they would fire me, because I was too naughty. But at that time I had started collecting records, even though I did not have a record player, so I played tapes, bootleg tapes. I would get bootleg tapes on Temple Street (in Yau Ma Tei) for HK$5 each, or three for HK$10. These were low-quality tapes that were cheap because I was poor. I tried to get as many as I could and to listen to as much as possible. Since I couldn't listen to my records, I would get friends to make recordings of them for me. Some of the first records were Grand Funk Railroad, Led Zeppelin, Deep Purple . . .

I was living on the rooftop of this very old, lousy

al

J

all time favourites
instrumental versions

includes:
ginny come lately
cindy oh cindy
look for a star
river of no return
and the sun will shine
my love for you & others
lyrics to all songs enclosed

radio hongkong 14001

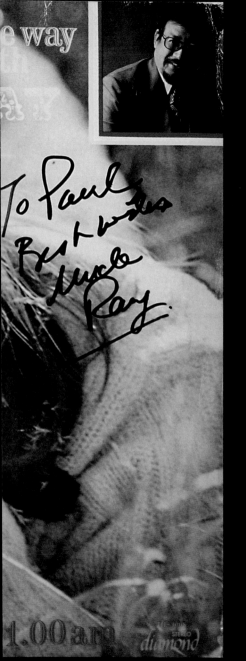

Sample Record #8:
All the Way with Ray

Paul: A promotional album from the legendary RTHK (Radio Television Hong Kong) disc jockey Ray Cordeiro (Uncle Ray) who came to my shop on December 8, 2012 for a co-interview about vinyl records on the day before his 88th birthday. The album is instrumental versions of well-known pop/rock hits done by local Hong Kong musicians. Uncle Ray is the leader of the Hong Kong Elvis Presley Fan Club and met Elvis in the United States. He also interviewed The Beatles in 1964, three times in one week just before they came to Hong Kong.

building, with rats and everything. There was no elevator. I had to walk up the stairs. It was a five-story building, and the fifth floor was the roof top. I was a squatter on the rooftop. I was trying to learn how to play drums but there was no place to set up drums there. We actually were living there illegally. A lot of people would just hide on this rooftop and put up a squat without the knowledge of the government. In fact, the landlord was my cousin, my mother's cousin's son.

On the ground floor there would be two numbers, two addresses, but the roof covered both addresses. Some squatters would be on one side of the building and we would be on the other. The shelters were like very small huts built out of sheet metal. My mother's mother and her relatives, when they fled China, went first to Macau and then to Hong Kong. They stayed in this same squat (in North Point, Hong Kong) from the 1950s to the 1970s. When I arrived the squat was all ready there. There was no air con or heat, and the weather was very hot and then very cold. It was lousy as hell. I tell you, in Hong Kong it is heaven for rich people and hell for the poor people. I was living in hell.

I lived there from '75 until '82. Then my cousin who owned the whole building sold it to some developers.

We got letters from lawyers telling us that we had to move out by the end of '82. So I had to look for another squat.

I started looking in the newspaper. People were selling rooftop squats. Some were very expensive, some were very lousy, some were up in the hills with no electricity and no toilet and they would throw the shit onto the hillside. Finally I found a squat near here in

Sham Shui Po (the district where Paul's Records is located), just four blocks from here, and I managed to buy it. Well, it's illegal but people would build them and then sell them. The owner of the building wouldn't get involved; sometimes the rooftop was common property. If they owned the rooftop they might call the police. But the squat I bought was not on the rooftop but

Paul (standing right) and his family in 1974

on the top of the stairway. The stairway had a cover and the squat was on top of the cover. It was very strange. I bought it for HK$20,000, which would be about HK$200,000 now. At that time I was only earning about HK$1000 a month. The squat was

about 100 square feet for HK$20,000. That wasn't a lot of money then. The regular apartment cost about HK$300,000 to buy, so I could not afford that. So I had no choice, and I just stayed there.

I got into this business (selling records) in 1983 when I moved to Sham Shui Po and I did not have a job. I started buying records for my own collection. Then I started selling my spare records on the street. I sold on the street so I did not have to pay rent (for a shop) and then I could use the money to buy more records. At that time I only had one or two boxes of records or about 200 records, but then I bought more records and two boxes became four, four boxes became six, and so on.

Every evening after I finished selling I would take all these boxes of heavy records up to the rooftop and then the next day back down to the street; then use a trolley to move them about four blocks. Finally it just got to be too many, so at the end of the day I just put them on the trolley and covered them with canvas and started sleeping on the street to watch them. From that time on I seldom went back to my place on the rooftop. My clothes and things were there, but I seldom went back there. I only went back about once a week. Most of the time I was on the street, on a 24-hour stand-by location, selling these records. I was like a cowboy who had to keep watch over his cattle.

I was always there on the street playing music loud. I used a car battery for electricity and I was playing records. People knew me because I was on the street. I did not have a cell phone or a pager, but people know that I would be there. I lived a very simple life, like a hippie. There were also a lot of used clothes dealers in the area, so I could find cheap clothes for myself. I ate very little and I paid no rent. I didn't travel much, had low or no transportation fees, so it was easy to live. I mainly spent money on the records, all of my money, each and every dollar, on the records. My customers became my friends so we traded information and I learned about music and records that way.

At that time people really didn't know my name. I had a long beard and I came to be known as "the bearded boy". I also had long hair, but it was so hot that I would tuck it up under my hat. Even in '86 people in Hong Kong hated long hair. They were much different than people are now, the older generation then hated me. They would say things in front of me like they didn't know if I was a boy or a girl. So in '86 they did not like me, and I hid my hair but I had grown a beard so they started calling me "the bearded boy". Not until 1990 did they start to know me as "Paul".

I sold records on the street until '92 and then I had saved some money and I got a small shop just down stairs from here. And then in 2003 I moved up to the fifth floor location. I moved up here because of the price of the rent and I was also having trouble with this fucking dentist who was my neighbor. I was selling at the location downstairs that is now selling Taiwan Bubble Tea. There was a dentist next door who kept complaining, "Hey, you can't play music here, you can't put your records out here!" And I just told them, "What are you talking about. This is the place for flea markets, this is for the people in Sham Shui Po, not for self-styled high-class dentists! You should go to Tsim Sha Tsui or something! It should be me stopping you, not you stopping me!" In fact I did not disturb him because he was doing his business inside and I was selling on the street. I don't know why but he was so fussy and he just treated me like a cockroach or whatever. The landlord had split the storefront in half and I just rented a cockloft (a small, low-ceiling space directly above a larger space) where I stored my records, but I sold them outside on the street. Finally the dentist got the landlord to ask me to leave and I moved up here.

Sample Record #9: Fung Bo Bo

Petrina Fung Bo Bo (馮寶寶) started her career as a child actress in 1960 and has since then exhibited a longevity not uncommon to the Hong Kong entertainment industry. Still active, though semi-retired, she has appeared extensively in both films and TV series, playing a full range of roles from precocious toddlers to edgy adults. Not surprisingly dubbed the "Shirley Temple of the East" by local media during that phase of her career, she was also prey to that star's similarly exhausting filmmaking schedule, which, for instance, saw the young Fung Bo Bo working on four films at once.

What is also common within the limits of the Hong Kong entertainment industry (not to mention the expectations placed upon someone com-

pared to Shirley Temple) is that she had a singing and recording career as well, which again runs the gamut from early-career good-girl didacticism (and the title on the single to the left can be translated as "Good Child - 好兒童") to covering the theme from M*A*S*H (in English) in 1970.

The single below is taken from the film "Social Characters" (1969) in which Bo Bo played a supporting role while apparently singing the title song. This film fits into a sub-genre of Hong Kong films that addressed wayward youth à la "Rebel Without a Cause", unsupervised youth that were seen to be prey to delinquency. The Cantonese title of the film literally translates to "Fly Boy, Fly Girl", a vernacular term for this type of dispossessed youngster.

Another Story:
Hong Kong Daily News, November 5, 1985

Paul has had many newspaper and magazine articles written about him in both the Chinese and English language Hong Kong print media (along with being interviewed by various TV shows). He is also the go-to-guy when someone in the media is looking for a specific title, particularly when it's something that was produced in Hong Kong.

The following article from The Hong Kong Daily News comes from the time when Paul was selling records and living on the streets of Sham Shui Po, taking care of his wares (as he puts it: like a cowboy watching his cattle).

The article is presented here to exemplify that there are more than two sides to every story, and to reveal the relative techniques of, and approaches to, journalism.

In the interests of completeness (and full disclosure) the article is first presented here in an English translation and then in the original Chinese.

社會寫貌

我選擇了鴨寮街！

新舊對比鮮明——自由浪漫開放

一個忠於自我的中年男人，面對一個成長了七件成長，其中一件另今社會仍然相處不妥協兩難，一邊是欣賞願意于賢桃園種桃花選，附和大多數者擇自我……

這是他一番的感觸，是賢對的判斷，可是他心裡亦明白，一幾個人不走鴨寮街的滄桑，有了那走不出我，但不想追思遠，說及社會對我，這是他心裡的思念……

就社會出口以時入陽寮街，是眼目前走是一個個賢陽我的人，一邊的思味是一件不一個的走，不一不同的人，細看在滄桑更思念，不賢的出個買賣的，有一些的思念，他的財賢的我不走走走賢滿走退感，在賢賢的動賣，一些之人我退思念的人我，計情選賣……

為之裡思個——另一個桃子圍滿了人，不看自其實成長我中和我，大批大批思我不是上我賢，我佔在一個男人，我的鬼腳鬮閃賢，一我的鬼腳腳看，我走一個手提花陽，一個手一則及賢那思賣得，聽走倒及賢那者一個思賣一而的走，說出思我拿思出走賣，把吐個賣我而即行走退，得一個個我而即行走退，得吐思賣賢即賣，照一了……

鴨寮街是過個不新的自由，法律、都取會付我思賢的能樂，是一個賢賣者那水行那，我是人特能我樂，要之地賣我思樂，要吃個起賢者我思即樂，我是一個即我的每的個思賢賣思走及走，法律不我，是一個個別法而思出，一賢個思樣賣我者的我，是一個個思即賢的走賣，多古樣很賢……

這就整理的全腿腿，可想賢那者出賣很賢即面的了……

拒絕庸俗卻甘與培塿為鄰

「髭鬚仔」——單純的執著者

攝片是他的命根，他那錢全花在攝片上，稱水浮有國標賣出多少米？

清證古賣文錦錄客思賣我，聽我即而思走。

梱片面賢賣的個新賢——思賢賣我賢那、一對賢走思個很思的思。

在這裡、兩個不不維地收錢、是一對思的個不我的思。

對命運不妥協的實幹者

白手興家「事頭婆」

電纜終於上軌道

生命力極強的女人

不為千元月薪所動

帶著八元隻身來港

策劃：龍景昌
編輯：陳約基
採訪：羅少蘭
攝影：鄭逸宇
設計：美術部

Translated from the
Hong Kong Daily News, November 5, 1985

Refuses to partner with vulgarity
but is willing to be a neighbor in low places

"The Bearded Guy" –
The Simple Persistent Man

If you walk from Nam Cheong Street to Ap Liu Street, you see market stalls on both sides of a very crowded street. On one corner, there is a stall unlike other stores; it is stocked with nicely arranged old vinyl records. Here you can find rock and roll, jazz, Cantonese Opera, as well as Chinese and western pop songs. One can easily tell that this is a rich collection.

Refuses to Grow Up – Contempt for Authority

This is the stall of Paul Au Tak Shing, "The Bearded Guy", who has been selling old records on Ap Liu

Street for over two years. When we met him he was wearing a dingy white shirt, a pair of raggedy blue jeans, a pair of rubber slippers, and a straw hat that holds his shoulder-length hair. His shirt was stained and his hands were dirty; maybe he hasn't showered for days. But the records are his life; the Woodstock spirit of the 1960s and "the fortress of the medieval warrior" are his utopias.

Paul knows that he is not accepted by the other shopkeep-ers on Ap Liu Street, but he doesn't con-cern himself-with what oth-ers despise.

He readily admits to being immature, as he can't ac-cept the reality of others; he refuses to "grow up", thinking that growing up makes one a snob. He wants to be a hippy, and sees his efforts and lifestyle as a silent protest. He doesn't pay attention to time or money, because he doesn't want to become buderned by them . . . and thus, he has spent a precious thirty years of his life pursuing his unique lifestyle.

Paul, the offspring of Chinese parents, grew up in Saigon's Chinatown and lived through the Vietnam War of the 1960s. This turned him into a lifelong pacifist. He confesses: "The Vietnam government was authoritarian and couldn't do much that was positive, there was so much corruption. The police and the soldiers did not care about the law and killed many people, and yet a lot of them could get away with it by bribing the officials. " Growing up in such environment, he became suspicious of authority.

在這裏，再沒有人騷擾他緬懷過去，尋求他的「胡士托精神」。

Here, no one interrupts him being melancholic about the past, or looking for his "Woodstock spirit".

Hated the War - Indulged in Music

He speaks very seriously: "When I was in middle school in Vietnam, the school hired some off-duty American soldiers to teach us English. Although they were at war in Vietnam, deep down they were against it. In the class they would say 'Get Out (of Vietnam) Kennedy!' and they often talked about how important peace, fraternity, dignity, equality and freedom really are. I was deeply moved and have since pursued absolute freedom. "

"The Bearded Guy" witnessed American soldiers drunk and high on drugs in the streets of Saigon, but he himself opted for the noisy rock and roll which became his driving passion; it acted as a protest against the times. Paul says, "When I was 15 or 16, I really responded to that music and I very much wanted to own those records."

At the end of 1974, the outcome of the war was becoming clear; the Communist army had almost succeeded in invading Saigon. This was just before Paul reached his eighteenth year. His mother was afraid that he would be recruited into the army and killed on the battlefield; through illegal channels she arranged for him to flee to Hong Kong. Paul was forced to say good-bye to his friends and family along with the local Vietnamese rock bands with whom he had spent so many hours. Feeling alone and helpless he boarded a freighter and crossed the ocean to Hong Kong. He would no longer be able to enjoy the music beaming from the American army's radio stations.

Paul continues, "My dad gave the smugglers 5 taels of

gold, which was his savings from his accountant job. After that he was left with almost nothing." Since he doesn't care for money any longer, he recounted all this with great effort.

One way journey to Hong Kong - Mind and heart are pressured

When he first arrived, Paul only had one relative in Hong Kong, an uncle. He lived with this uncle for seven years, even though he didn't get along with him. He moved out at the end of 1982. "During those 7 years, I had many jobs but I was never happy. Until today, I still dream that I have clocked in 1 minute late to work and the boss is yelling at me. That still makes me feel bad." Longing to establish his own lifestyle, he didn't work at all in 1984.

Eventually, "The Bearded Guy" wandered through Ap Liu Street, and after 12 years in Hong Kong, he found his "Xanadu". Paul explains, "The way Ap Liu Street operates is very interesting. In this rich city, a lot of things are thrown away without being fully utilized, which is big waste. Here in Ap Liu Street, a lot of vendors sell second-hand items to people who need them." He giggles, "In fact, humans can have low demand for material. Whether the clothes are new or old, they work fine as long as they cover the body; however the food tastes, it is best if it can fill the stomach; and sleeping outdoors makes one feel close to nature. The most important thing is to have an abundant spiritual life, a personal hobby and not to let one's ideals be buried."

The Bearded Guy sometimes has to face trouble from the real world, for example, drug users often deliberately harass him, which is difficult for him to deal with.

Orphan of the times? Don Quixote?

In fact, he has found the ragged and old atmosphere that he dreamed of. Here, no one can interrupt him from ruminating on the melancholic "Woodstock spirit". He has finally built a spiritual fortress, making it a shelter that protects him from the harshness of society. But he nonchalantly admits that he is living in the past.

Even though he doesn't care about what is normal or average to most people, he sometimes comes face to face with the harshness of the real world on the streets of Sham Shui Po; local drug addicts harass him and he must adapt to their denigrating habits.

But in the end, he loves his records, spending all his money buying more, reluctant to even sell one. He has even been having a hard time paying the rent for a nearby two hundred square feet attic where he stores his collection.

"The Bearded Guy", someone who refuses to "grow up", someone who shows little care for financial matters - what does the future hold for him?

拒絕庸俗卻甘與培塿為鄰
「鬍鬚仔」-- 單純的執著者

從南昌街轉入鴨寮街，左右展開兩排攤檔，街上行人如常地摩肩接踵，熙熙攘．街尾轉角處，擺賣着排列有序、各式各樣的舊唱片，跟其他舊唱片攤檔的雜亂很不一樣，那裡有樂與怒、爵士、粵曲、也有中西流行曲，一看便知道是一個很豐富的收藏。

拒絕成長‧蔑視權威

鬍鬚仔在鴨寮街賣舊唱片已經有兩年多,這次決定與他詳談時,他身穿白襯衫及褪了色的牛仔褲,腳踏膠拖鞋,頭戴草帽,將及肩的頭髮全納於帽內,但卻仍零落地垂下了一兩條吋許長的粗髮,灰灰白白的襯衫呈現烏漬斑斑,十個指頭都鑲了厚實的黑泥,想他已有多天沒洗澡了。這些他都不重視、不在乎,唱片、樂與怒才是他的命根;六十年代的胡士托精神才是他的理想;「中世紀武士的堡壘」才是他的烏托邦。

鬍鬚仔雖自知不為人所接受,但對別人鄙視的眼光卻滿不在乎。他自認不成熟,因為自覺不能接受現實;他拒絕「成長」,認為成長只會帶來滿身俗氣,他要做嬉皮士,認為這是對勢利社會的一種無形控訴;他不重視時間與金錢,因為他們容易使人便成奴隸……如此這般地,他已渡過了人生極寶貴的三十個年頭。

鬍鬚仔生於越南華僑家庭,在西貢市附近的唐人街長大。六十年代越戰爆發,小小年紀便經歷了戰火的洗禮,腦海裏充滿了反戰思想。他憶述說:「越南政府很專制無能,貪污事件泛濫,警察及軍人目無法紀,動輒開鎗殺人,罪犯卻可籍賄賂官員逍遙法外。」在這樣混亂的政治環境下長大,難怪鬍鬚仔養成了蔑視權威的反叛性格。

厭恨戰爭‧沉醉音樂

「在越南唸中學時,學校請來一些休假的美軍教授英語。雖然他們身在越南作戰,骨子裏卻是絕對反戰的。課堂上他們滿口

『甘迺迪滾蛋』，時常宣揚和平、友愛、人類尊嚴、平等、自由。我深深地被感動，自此便開始對絕對自由的追尋。」他認真的說。

越戰扭曲了無數的心靈，也改變了很多人的生活態度。鬍鬚仔眼見無數美軍醉倒街頭、吸食毒品，他自己卻選擇了鬧哄哄的搖滾樂，藉以渲洩心中的激情、作出對時代的控訴。「十五、六歲時，我對這些音樂很有共鳴，深深愛上了它，很想擁有這些唱片。」鬍鬚仔說。

七四年末，戰局逐漸明朗，共軍幾乎攻入西貢。當時鬍鬚仔快年滿十八歲，母親恐怕愛兒被徵召入伍，成為炮灰，遂着令他偷渡往香港。於是，他告別了兒時朋友，以及共處多時的搖滾樂隊伙伴，帶著一份無奈的心情隻身登上貨輪，漂洋過海直奔香港，再也不能欣賞美軍電台的音樂廣播了。

「爸爸給了蛇頭付了五両黃金，大約值越幣一百萬元（折合港幣五千），是他多年來當會計的積蓄，付欵以後，他亦所餘無幾了。」一向不重視金錢數目的鬍鬚仔吃力地算着。

投奔怒海‧心靈受壓

大舅父是鬍鬚仔在港唯一的親人，起初七年，他寄住在舅父家裡。寄人籬下的他與舅父的感情並不好，雖然盡力忍耐遷就，直到八二年末，還是決定遷出。「這七年間，我輾轉做過多份職業，總是不愜意。直到今天，我仍然常夢見自己返工時打咭遲了一分鐘，被老闆大罵。有時夢見小時後功課未做好，被老是當眾指責，很是難受。」他既追求絕對自由，又受不了時間限制與壓力，所以在八四年整整一年沒有工作。

在偶然的機會下，鬍鬚仔閒蕩到鴨寮街，竟找到他偷渡來港十二年的「世外桃源」。「鴨寮街的作息是挺有意思的，在這富裕城市裏，很多東西都未曾物盡其用，浪費得很，鴨寮街的攤販則可將被遺棄的東西轉售與有需要的人。」他帶着傻笑地說，「其實，人對物資的需求可以很低，衣服不論新舊欵式，可蔽體便行；飲食不論什麼味道，可裹腹便為佳；露天而睡使我更接近大自然。最重要的，是精神生活豐足，個人興趣與理想不被埋沒」

時代遺孤？唐吉訶德？

事實上，鴨寮街的殘舊氣氛是他夢寐以求的。在這裏，沒有人騷擾他緬懷過，尋求他的「胡士托精神」，他終於能建立了一座精神上的堡壘，作為與現實社會的屏障。鬍鬚仔亦淡然承認，他是活在過往的。

「流浪漢、野人、嬉皮士、不懂自愛……」不接受鬍鬚仔的人總喜歡用帶有挑剔性的字眼形容他。不容否認，在一個如香港般富裕的社會，人人穿着趨時，又怎能容得下髮長及肩、滿面于思、衣衫襤褸、滿身塵埃的「鬍鬚仔」呢？

"Tramp, savage, hippy, self-hater…" those who don't accept "The Bearded Guy" use these harsh words to describe him. In an affluent city like Hong Kong, where everyone follows the trends, how can they accept his shoulder-length hair, bearded face, ragged clothes, and dirty appearance?

不過，不食人間煙火的鬍鬚仔有時也要面對現實的困擾，例如隔鄰攤檔的道友常惡意侵犯，是他感到難於應付。而且，因為他愛「碟」成癖，把錢全花在唱片上，又捨不得賣出去，以致半年未有付交那二百來呎裝放唱片的閣樓租金，正面臨被逼遷的煩惱。對於前面要走的路，不善理財而又拒絕「成長的」鬍鬚仔，將會如何抉擇？

Many thanks to the *Hong Kong Daily News*
for permission to reprint this article

Sample Record #10a:
Sheung Kwun Lau Wan （上官流雲）

曲小語粵

啦 的 快 行
CAN'T BUY ME LOVE
人 玉 想 心 一
I SAW HER STANDING THERE
梨 沙 鹹
唱雲流官上

HBEP 185

Paul: A Singaporean two-hit wonder, very big in Southeast Asia in the 1960s. This is two Beatles hits covered in Singaporean Cantonese with only a Beatles' sing-a-long instrumental record for his background music. His lyrics sound like some of the original English words but have a different meaning in Cantonese.

行快啲啦 (the remake of "Can't Buy Me Love) actually means "Walk Faster" and is a commentary on the fast speed of life in Singapore at that time.

一心想玉人 (the remake of "I Saw Her Standing There") mimics the sound of the English in Cantonese, but he is actually singing "Thinking About My Princess"

粵語流行曲

行快的啦

一心想玉人

顧耶魯唱

百麗唱片公司出品

BAL

BL-21

What can the copyright holder do when presented with a bootleg copy of a bootleg? The pictured appropriation is a flexi-disc of the previous 45rpm that covered two Beatles songs with adapted Cantonese lyrics. But the "bootleg" of the "hit" is itself lifted from the "original bootleg" and reproduced on an unauthorized flexi-disc. This "cover song" has gone through so many filters that we can almost categorize it as "folk music", albeit one affected by advanced technologies.

The motorcycles

When I first came to Hong Kong, I couldn't afford anything. I was finally able to buy a Harley (Harley-Davidson motorcycle) in 1991. I was still selling records on the street but I was able to save some money. It had been my dream to buy a "chopper" since 1973, because we saw people in magazines riding them, people like Janis Joplin and Jimi Hendrix, and we knew about the Hell's Angels (American motorcycle club) and the movie, "Born To Be Wild", which I didn't

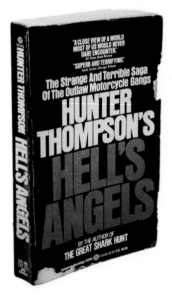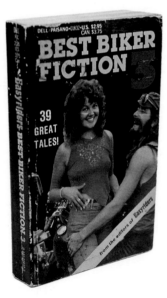

From Paul's biker book collection

see until '76 in Hong Kong on TV, even though it had played in Saigon before that. Also, we saw the "choppers" on the American TV show "The Mod Squad", maybe in '71 or '72.

Objects on a shelf in Paul's Sham Shui Po shop

I had heard about this Harley club in Hong Kong run by an Italian-American guy. In late 1989 there was an article in the South China Morning Post about him and he was trying to find people with similar interests. So he met this one guy, a German working in a bank in Hong Kong, and they started the club. They would just get junky bikes and work on them. No one in Hong Kong really knew about Harleys. Everyone only knew about the Japanese bikes. I eventually bought my Harley from one of the American

Paul in full biker regalia (1990)

One of Paul's many half-sized motorcycles in his Tuen Mun storage space

Embassy staff members. He had had it shipped over here from the U.S. It was a 1989 model, one of only two in Hong Kong.

In 1990 I talked to the guy at the Hong Kong Harley motorcycle club and he told me they were looking for people who enjoyed Harleys. They would have parties, BBQs, at the American Embassy staff residence on Shouson Hill Road (in south side Hong Kong Island) and I showed up in my heavy metal gear and they were very impressed. At that time I didn't even have a license for driving a motorcycle, but I got one in 1991 and bought the Harley as I had met the owner at one of these parties. I would go for a midnight ride on my own or with the club on Sunday mornings. I stored it in a space in Sham Shui Po with some of my records. The Harley was a stock bike, not a "chopper", which was the motorcycle that I really wanted, so I sold the Harley 11 years later, in 2002, because my record collection was getting bigger and bigger.

Tuen Mun Storage Space

Paul is a hoarder, but his social role is also that of an archivist. After visiting his ramshackle shop a few times, he told me he not only had these records, but he also had a storage space in Tuen Mun full of other records. I began to consider the Tuen Mun storage space as the final bit of information that I needed to gather; possibly a holy grail, more than likely a simple but essential detail.

When the metal grates were finally pulled back in the corridors outside Paul's Tuen Mun storage space, in an industrial building permeated with oily residue, humidity and dust, I beheld a thousand square feet crammed with box upon box of records and playback equipment (mostly in the form of turntables). The first thing I said was, "I had no idea".

Paul is dedicated to this eccentric museum which has a simple focus (any and every pre-digital analog recording that he comes across).

But his dedication is also based on a complex mixture of nostalgia (creating a tangible connection to his past) and a concern for the environment. He frequently decries the consumerist trends of Hong Kong people, who are quick to throw away recently expired products.

Paul connects this specific brand of environmentalism with an idealized "hippie" ethic, the Rock n' Roll role model of his teenage years. Paul wants to save all the records destined for the dump. He makes deals

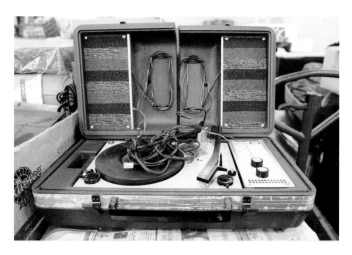

with DJs who have decided to go digital, he goes to record shop closing sales, and he buys, sight unseen, boxes of records from Japan.

The storage space is obviously filled with buried treasure, along with multiple never-opened albums of "cheesy", low-budget, pop piano music. I want to be left alone for a few days to sort it all out and eventually walk away with the results of my extensive archeology. Paul does make allowances for the occa-

Sample Record #11: Grand Funk Railroad

It's appropriate to at least include one selection dedicated to the Rock and Roll influences that got Paul started on his record buying and selling journey, represented here by the American band, Grand Funk Railroad, a group important to many American Vietnam veterans because of, for one thing, the lyrics for "I'm Your Captain (Closer to Home)" which became an allusion to the morass of the Vietnam War and the desire of the frontline soldier to return home.

Paul: I got some of that influence because of the long-hair Vietnamese bands, and they covered a lot of the Grand Funk Railroad songs. The best Vietnamese cover band when I was a teenager in Saigon was CBC (led by two siblings, Nam Loc and her brother, Tung Linh). They had two girls singing the parts that Mark Farner would do on the records.

Some of the street stalls in Saigon sold a lot of things stolen from the American Army PX, all kinds of things, like brandy, records, tapes, magazines. I was too poor to buy anything but my rich friend was always looking for records to buy. I would go along because I wanted to learn more about the music. We would always find something.

In 1972 my father finally bought a record player, it was like a "James Bond" device - a turntable, cassette player and radio all in a small suitcase. That was my very first turntable. But we really didn't have any records, just a few Taiwanese bootlegs. Plus the sound wasn't very good. My friend had a big stereo system, a Pioneer turntable, Sony cassette deck, a Sony open reel tape recorder, and very big speakers. He was also buying the original American and British rock albums. One day I went over and he was playing Grand Funk Railroad, and I was like, "Wah! What is that?" He showed me the record cover, it was the first Grand Funk Railroad album, "On Time" (from 1969). That was the first real hard rock and roll that I had heard, the song from that album called, "Are You Ready". I went very close to the speakers and the punch of the drum was very hard and I just fell in love with the heavy metal. I would learn about those bands from him and he would loan me the albums and I would make cassette recordings on my father's "James Bond" stereo.

My friend and I would also see advertisements for Grand Funk Railroad in the music magazines smuggled out of the American Army PX store, magazines like Circus or Hit Parader. We would sometimes find magazines that didn't sell in the PX that were supposed to be returned to the distributor; they would tear off the covers of these magazines and give them to a recycler. My friend and I would go to the paper recycler and get some of those magazines. There was one issue from 1973, and there was a picture with Mark Farner on a horse, acting like a native-American and the article said he wanted to come to Vietnam and play for the G.I.s. Of course we wouldn't be allowed to go to that concert, and anyhow, those concerts would be closer to where the Americans were fighting, somewhere like Da Nang.

Mark Farner came to Hong Kong in 1983 to lead a guitar clinic and I had a chance to talk to him and he told me that they hadn't been allowed to play in Vietnam because they were blacklisted, because they were singing songs like "People, Let's Stop the War".

Once I started collecting records in Hong Kong I bought those three Grand Funk Railroad albums for myself, in fact, I have double copies of some. They are not so easy to find in Hong Kong, as the record label in Hong Kong at that time was promoting Deep Purple more than Grand Funk Railroad, maybe because Deep Purple was British. When I started looking for records, there were Deep Purple records everywhere.

sional "DJ Crew" who wants to engage in an all-night crate digging session.

At that moment, I didn't have the time or inclination for a thorough search. My mission was to photograph the storage space, but nevertheless, I did thumb through the occasional attractive pile, pulling out something that had winked at me through the rubble.

Besides the object's original intention, that of a freshly produced and priced-for-sale record, most of these records are now used items, still on the market (what we call "the secondary market") but now imbued with another level of information. They carry traces of the original owner; mysterious incomplete stories of their purpose, use, and relative value. These qualities are actually disparaged by the professional collector, who seeks the most pristine and undamaged artifact possible. The hand-written name of the original owner (or any other information that alters the original packaging) is seen as a liability, something that will lower the resale value.

But if we are really building a museum (with this book as a guide) this tangential, overlooked and devalued information adds something of consequence.

These stray markings, like any other historically obscured information, also require some kind of expert, someone with a background in our subject (records and record collecting), someone who can distinguish if the previous owner was French or Japanese, or if the markings indicate private or corporate ownership. Otherwise, we are free to ruminate on these disconnected references; we will rely on our intuition as we fondle the tactile object; we wonder about another time (perhaps long ago) and place (perhaps far away) when another set of hands in another building played this very record.

For instance, as I moved around the storage space looking for the right image or the correct angle, a box of 45rpms caught my attention. The labels and titles coincided with my proclivities, with my taste in music. The 45rpms leaned towards "funk music", with titles that clearly exhorted the listener to dance. I called out to Paul that I thought I had found something and picked out a few singles with lesser-known labels. After I had handled them for a while, turned them over from A side to B side, I realized that the box had once been the property of a Japanese Disco DJ. This was, it seemed, the unknown DJ's entire stock (from the late 70s), filling a box with enough titles to propel a full night of dancing.

This conclusion was garnered from scraps of paper that had been taped to the singles, in Japanese and English, that listed the title and some kind of code (either for cataloging or rating). Their use in a disco was confirmed by a large "A" that had been written

on the side of each record that was meant for the turntable, thus allowing the DJ to be quick in the low-lit confines of a nightclub. All of the records had been produced in the United States, but had a feature that I had never seen before on 7- inch records – each side held the same song, but the flipside was either a longer "Disco Version", or a "Part 2" instrumental.

At one time this box of 45rpm 7-inch singles had been an integral part of the business of pleasure, perhaps a secret weapon in the Japanese Disco wars, but it was now sitting in Paul's Tuen Mun storage space bereft of its everyday use, yet still maintaining its potential as didactic material. Paul had no idea how he had ended up with the intact box, and this missing piece of information might have allowed us to connect the dots – who was the DJ (and where is he/she now), what kind of club were the records played in (a small private members-only club or a Yakuza-run mega-Disco), and were the venue's clients genuine cogno-

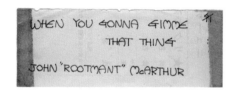

scenti or blasé, drunken office workers? Many actual museums are also burdened by unavoidable gaps in their historical narratives, gaps that are sometimes filled with theoretical speculation.

We do know how to play a record, but due to personal biases we are usually attracted to one song and not another. It is precisely the implied narrative represented by this box of 45rpms, and the historical context that it represents as a cultural artifact, that makes our interest in it go beyond simple "taste". We are being given a glimpse of a previously unknown spot.

Given the rich yet incomplete information that Paul's archive presents, we may also take on the guise sometimes assumed when one is in the process of rummaging through another's property – that of a snoop; someone who is searching for some gossip.

From Paul's collection of unusual playback devices - a Sky Studio portable record player from 1983

These then, given the context of this entire project, are the opposing terms: archivist versus hoarder, compiler of valuable information versus snoop; the socially accepted as opposed to the possibly outcast.

And as far as the records themselves, it becomes a matter of their ranking as cherished object or useless trash. Who will save this pile of trash (just as the archeologist will dig through an ancient town's dump)?

Given all the stuff we have now accumulated, all the materials that are continuously lost and found, Paul well demonstrates the contemporary circumstance wherein the consumer becomes a kind of producer, someone involved in a self-designated creative pursuit.

My own role can then be proposed as interpreter, someone who was presented with the product and the producer, the collected and the collector, and as in Marcel Duchamp's theory of artistic self-designation, has named them art and artist.

Sample Record #12: "All for Freedom" by Lowell Lo

"All for Freedom" was produced and recorded in Hong Kong in support of the 1989 student occupation of Beijing's Tiananmen Square. Recorded on May 23, 1989, the song was hand-delivered and broadcast in Tiananmen Square the next day, on May 24. The song is unusual as, in addition to its well-noted political content, it incorporates both Cantonese and Putonghua (Mandarin) lyrics and has a harder Rock sound than most Canto-Pop songs.

There are two versions of the song, one a choral version  and another longer version that utilizes 150 Canto-Pop singers (the style of Hong Kong or Cantonese Pop) creating Hong Kong's take on "We Are the World" - a benefit recording in support of a social / political cause. The song's narrative and legacy might also epitomize "Hong Kong culture", with its typical mix of the artistic, the political and the commercial.

Written by Lowell Lo (盧冠廷), a respected Hong Kong song writer and performer (dubbed the "Hong

Kong Bob Dylan") who has since gone on to a career in environmental activism, the song became a smash hit in Hong Kong, entering the Hong Kong pop charts in the last week of May 1989, and becoming the number one song for the first three weeks of June.

The paradox of the political becoming pop (and hence, commercial) meant that the recording companies, who had some of the 150 singers under contract, became contentious about the disbursement of the recording's royalties, and how much of a showcase any particular artist would get within the huge roster of talent.

Media hype had surrounded the recording and its release from the beginning, with fans flocking to the studio when the "all-star" recording took place. The popular response eventually resulted in a star studded concert and television broadcast in support of the Mainland democracy movement.

The intent of "All for Freedom" was clearly sincere, more than timely, and the rights (and profits) to the song were eventually allocated to the Hong Kong Alliance, a pro-democracy group still in existence. But it becomes hard, in this case, to separate commercial ambition from the political will of the performers. Paul reported, when lending this cassette, that it is now a collector's item, fetching up to HK$1000 (or about US$130).

But the specific historical context of this recording should also be clearly noted. Not only was the Tiananmen Square crack down a murderous denial to any potential opposition to the Chinese Communist Party, but Hong Kong, while still a British Colony at this point in time had, through extensive negotiations that concluded in 1984, been ceded to the Mainland (to be "handed-over" in 1997). It can be surmised that this was a high point for anti-Beijing/pro-democracy sentiment amongst a majority of Canto-Pop stars.

"When I first moved up here there was lots of room, not like it is now."

The Holy Grail

Please keep in mind that in any documentary or narrative project there is much that happens off-screen, mundane or integral details that are left unposted. And by doubling the project's categories, I reveal that I am up-in-the-air about a precise genre, a conundrum all too common to our era.

There is a story, but off-screen, or in the complete unedited tapes, there are a lot of other things happening, conversations and pauses, temporal items that are less condensed than a movie or a song. The obvious suppressed element of these out-takes are: boredom, un-excitement, or perhaps what we concisely call "everyday life".

Over the period of my investigation I became friends with Paul and at times the length of my visits far exceeded the information that I gathered, or I became involved in pursuits beyond the scope of this book. Paul and I also talked about (among other things) politics, our visits to other countries, the price of real estate and rental property, and the owners and locations of other used record stores in Hong Kong. Usually, regardless of my intention, a visit would elicit some piece of provocative information that could or could not be incorporated into the project.

The "everyday life" quality of my visits was unlike my relationship with any other record store or record storeowner. "Paul's Records", within a specific realm, became part of my social life. I extracted the information and then Paul would introduce me to a new Vietnamese sandwich shop in the neighborhood. And like other investigations, or archeological digs, the longer one waits, the more time one has, the more likely one is to stumble across "something".

A very unusual (by western standards) Japanese 45rpm sleeve, and in excellent condition, nevertheless, it held a quite insipid moldy-oldy hit recording, "Sucu-Sucu" by Nina and Frederik. When I found and expressed interest in this sleeve, I declined to buy it after hearing its tedious jingle, but Paul insisted that I take it, " . . . because no one else would be interested in it". In other words, he wanted me to archive and take care of this artifact.

This "something", in relation to record collecting in Hong Kong, would hopefully be something unique to the region, a style of music or artist previously un-known or unheard of. But the non-Chinese speaker and/or reader who is solely reliant on his or her intu-ition is faced with the depth of an incomprehensible catalog and falls prey to a selection based on packag-ing. Most of the time, what is available in the used record store (or junk shop) is quite common regard-less of its colorful wrapping, the hit-of-the-moment recording produced in large enough quantities to eventually saturate the secondary market.

But this "worth" is relative to those who are search-ing for an artifact. What is common to one location might be exotic to another: a foreign script embedded on a color-saturated sleeve. And if I speak of the rela-tive definitions of exoticism and/or waiting around for "something" to come around the bend, how is it that I eventually found "That Makes Two of Us" by Merle Haggard and Bonnie Owen in a used cardboard box in Sham Shui Po, something that I hadn't even come close to smelling in the United States?

The vinyl record (like the book) is a tangible artifact, probably one reason for their continuing viability. People desire to hold the object in their hands, let alone that objects bear traces, seen or unseen, of the places and times that they came from. We hold or peruse the object, absorb its clues, and let our minds wander. The relative price or rarity of any given artifact points to an individual aesthetic, more so than to an actual value, and in this way the record collector can avoid the hyper-inflation of the contemporary art market while still amassing a visual display.

I had spent enough time at Paul's, waited around long enough, sifted through countless boxes, until one day he confessed to me, ". . . this stupid customer was looking for some Shanghai Jazz . . . there is no such thing . . . but I showed (him/her) this . . ." The desired item was a ten-inch Taiwanese bootleg of one of the purveyors of the so-called "Shanghai Style".

Shanghai, far before Hong Kong, was the modern media/entertainment capital of the Asian region, beginning from the development of sound and image recording technologies up until communist control of mainland China in the 1950s. That era now projects a curious mixture of western imperialism and privilege, the paradoxes of incorporating western culture into a modern Chinese identity, outright regional gangster-ism and sincere nationalist struggles, along with all the other aspects of a vibrant but decadent urban milieu.

Though there were an abundance of nightclubs during that time which featured jazz, jazz being the cultural export of the moment, some of the more pertinent western influences on the "Shanghai divas" were mainstream American vocalists like Deanna Durbin and Jeanette MacDonald, which points to the pervasive influence of film, a medium that was more widely accessible than the potentially exclusive nightclub. Many of the top singing stars of Shanghai at that time also moved between films and audio recordings, a circumstance that still exists today among Hong Kong entertainers.

The style of music then should not be referred to exclusively as "Jazz", and has more consistently been referred to in English as "Shanghai Style" and in Chinese Shi Dai Qu, which tellingly can be translated as "songs of the times" or less literally, "modern music". But this term was not in common usage in Shanghai during those years and the stated genre on any particular recording might in fact refer to jazz. Jazz was in the air, was of the times, was saturating the very pace of the city and influencing every ear open to "what's happening", to such an extent that trumpet player par excellence, Buck Clayton, future member of Count Basie's orchestra and then a collaborator in smaller bands with the iconic saxophonist Lester Young, was, in 1934, hired to lead one of Shanghai's many house bands.

It was jazz's syncopation and beat that was impossible to avoid as a contemporary influence, a factor that was also influencing American popular music at that time. But once the Shanghai recording industry took off, and though the record company of note was the British-owned Pathé label, a local market blossomed (seeing as the city's population was, despite the international concessions, vastly Chinese). This "style" then featured Chinese composers who began to incorporate indigenous instrumentation and well-known folk melodies into their songs.

China (as you should know) is a huge country, and this specific Shanghai moment is but a speck in its history, yet one that provokes us due to its multi-cultural ambiance and socioeconomic intrigues, a situation familiar to many contemporary cities. But in a case that might be compared with the continent of Africa, which has produced (and continues to produce) a gigantic trove of recorded music, the native English speakers of Europe and America hardly know where to begin in terms of "Chinese music", especially as far as modern or contemporary styles.

One point of entry into "Chinese music" (for the non-native speaker) was the 2005 CD release of "Shanghai Lounge Divas", a project that "remixed" songs by (among others) Chow Hsuan and Bai Kwong. This compilation garnered a surprising amount of sales by putting a post-Hip-Hop or dance music gloss onto Shi Dai Qu "classics", and while this produced a certain amount of perfunctory interest which saw these "remixes" broadcast in the trendy bars and lounges of Hong Kong, the original recordings have always been available in one form or another.

Why does any one piece (or genre) of music speak to you? Styles are adapted to make them more accessible for the average listener, or one is referred to an easily-gained point of departure. Jazz itself has spun off more or less popular sub-genres, has been watered down and diluted for those less inclined to its more esoteric or "savage" qualities. Who could have ever predicted that I would be attracted to a style partially based on the qualities of a singer like Jeanette MacDonald, who even in my youth appeared to be utterly passé?

"Shanghai Style" had long been on my radar (along with Canto-Pop, or any other of the stated local genres that I repeatedly came across) a term to be investigated rather than necessarily loved or appreciated. It was an off-hand comment by Paul that started the archeological dig in earnest, along with the quality of the product's packaging – a degraded and cheap bootleg, something usually avoided by the serious collector, a product that usurped copyright control, and in its very generic and rushed aesthetic exposed something to my interest.

Taiwan (along with Hong Kong) has a long and curious history of by-passing the entrenched legal strictures common to the European and American markets. There are longstanding products in Hong Kong, such as the cheap and low-resolution two-disc VCDs that innocently bootleg Hollywood blockbusters (or duds). The scale of this market and the futility of closing-the-barn-door-after-the-horse-has-bolted has seen a stopgap attempt to limit this market to certain regions of Asia. Taiwan was responsible, particularly in the 1960s and 70s, for countless twelve-inch LPs of western rock, pop, soul (you name it), sometimes in a picture sleeve that unintentionally brings to mind an Andy Warhol silkscreen with its arty misregistration of one of its color layers.

The ten-inch Taiwanese bootlegs of Shi Dai Qu lower the bar even further by packaging them in all-purpose sleeves that simply post the issuing company's name and logo. The sleeve itself is actually a plastic bag into which one piece of thin folded cardboard is inserted, thereby eliminating the need for binding the cardboard or providing an inner envelope. To top off the novel quality of these throw-away artifacts, the vinyl record is sometimes a stunning shade of orange or red.

Paul, in one of his erratic but sincere impulses to save the uncared-for recording, extracts the folded piece of cardboard, discards the original but now grimy plastic bag and supplies me with pristine clear-plastic inner and outer sleeves. He has had these custom-made (which he proudly recounted to me on more than one occasion, while decrying those who had appropriated this innovation). Finally, in his role as much-needed informant, he writes the

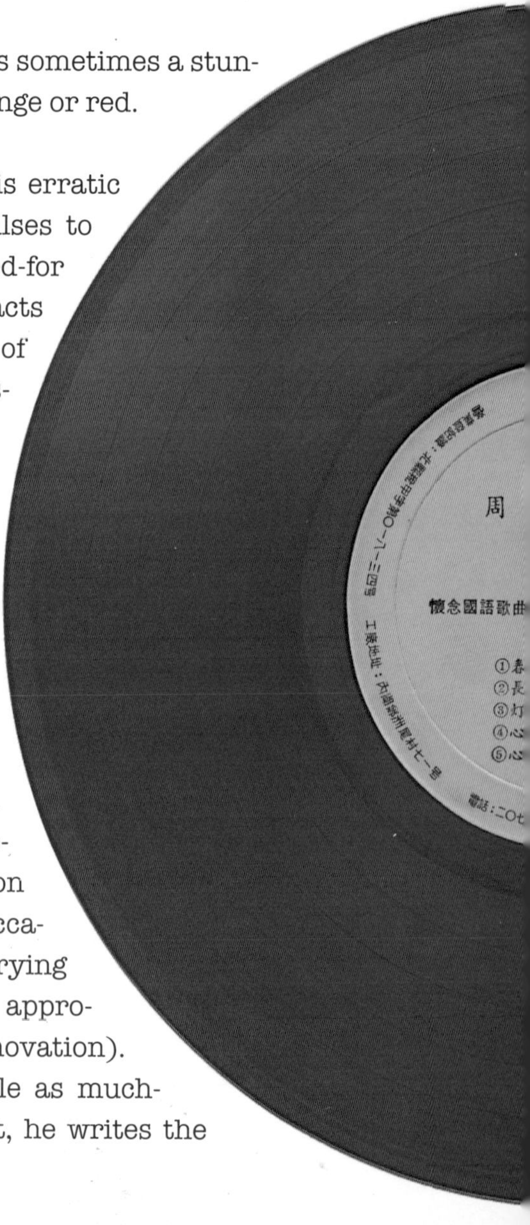

周

懷念國語歌曲

① 春
② 長
③ 燈
④ 心
⑤ 心

given artist's name in English and Chinese characters on the outer plastic sleeve.

The task of the non-native speaker is not only to recognize the sound of the word but to memorize its graphic shape. It is more proper to call the Chinese writing characters, as my letters are phonetic. For me, it becomes a matter of comparison, comparing two character shapes for similarities, but there is still confusion in the English transliteration (pinyin), as there may not be a comparable sound in English. We can achieve a relative cultural balance by recognizing

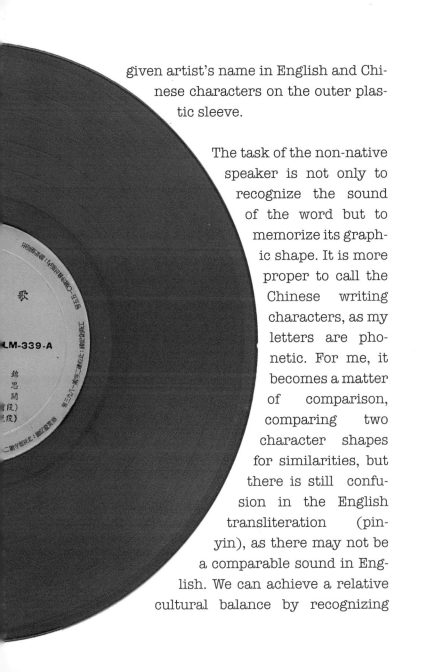

that the sound also changes if the spoken language is Mandarin or Cantonese, as Zhou Xuan (in Shanghai) might be Chow Hsuan (in Hong Kong), or 周璇 to both of them.

Zhou Xuan is a stage name. Zhou Xuan is a singer and film actress who worked in Shanghai and Hong Kong. She is one of the original outstanding three, an elite that will eventually become seven, a set pantheon that encompasses that era.

The story says that she was an orphan, a child sold off by an opium-addicted relative, raised as a Wang, in training as a courtesan, and then adopted as a Zhou. Eventually the title Xuan was assumed – meaning "jade" in Chinese. Beautiful jade.

She made over 40 movies and recorded over 200 songs, her most famous film being "Street Angel", a title that indicates the zeitgeist – streets and those who can remain an angel.

Just as Shanghai was rife with all the degradation and opulence that makes for the modern metropolis, Zhou Xuan also embodies the foibles of contemporary stardom, a highly successful type who is nevertheless prey to bouts of personal instability - unsuccessful love affairs, illegitimate children, and suicide attempts.

And now . . . stop for a moment, put aside the biographical influence, open your ears and listen to her song (many of the Shanghainese songs of this era are easy to find online; the Zhou Xuan film "Street Angel" is available on a public domain website).

花样的年华 (Hua Yang De Nian Hua) or "Mood for Love" or all the other literal or implied meanings of the Chinese title will be the chosen song (the song of choice) whether or not one deduces the influence of the western Pop and Jazz standard "I'm in the Mood for Love" in 花样的年华 or what it all has to do with the Wong Kar Wai film of the same title.

It doesn't matter if the language is foreign, unfamiliar to you, it is the distinctive sound, the tenor of the voice, its emotive power, that is speaking to you (that you are responding to). It is the very foreignness of the dialect that adds to this distinction, that moves the song (the singer) beyond her western influence, making the style her own.

She just opens her mouth, or plays the European instrument under the brow of her experience, and it comes out naturally, an artifact of a particular time and a specific place. All you have to do is to remember this - you need to listen to it more than once, now, or ten years from now, here, or in some other place.

亞洲唱片

唱片售出概不退換

Special thanks for research materials
and/or references:

Streets: Exploring Kowloon
by Jason Wordie

*All for Freedom: The Rise of Patriotic/Pro-Democracy
Popular Music in Response
to the Chinese Student Movement*
by Joanna Ching-Yun Lee

*Shanghai's Dancing World: Cabaret Culture
and Urban Politics, 1919-1954*
by Andrew Field

Age of Shanghainese Pops, 1930-1970
By Wong Kee Chee

Special thanks for permission to use images
and/or text:

Ray Cordeiro (Uncle Ray)
Hong Kong Daily News
Hong Kong Alliance
Petrina Fung Bo Bo
Universal Music Group (Capitol Records)

Special thanks for aid and support to:

Paul Au Tak Shing
Bing Czeng (translation)
William Fung

And most especially to Katrien Jacobs,
who provided everything necessary
for the completion of a creative project

EXPLORE ASIA WITH BLACKSMITH BOOKS
From retailers around the world or from *www.blacksmithbooks.com*

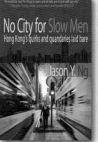

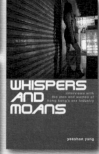

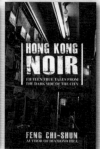